RAND'S AXIOM PROBLEM: ON OBJECTIVITY, ONTOLOGY, ESSENCE, EPISTEMOLOGY, DEDUCTION, INDUCTION, AND THE FOUNDATIONS OF KNOWLEDGE

Russell Hasan

CONTENTS

INTRODUCTION TO RAND'S AXIOM PROBLEM

The purpose of this paper is to analyze and solve problems in Ayn Rand's epistemology, particularly Rand's theory of axioms. Her main problem is that she fails to offer proof of the axiomatic propositions, which I believe can be debated and denied and are therefore in need of proof, so that Rand's epistemological foundation has a hole in it where a proof of the axioms should be. I will challenge Rand's intrinsic-objective-subjective analysis and posit that a theory of essences intrinsic in reality is necessary to prove identity and existence and to support a theory of reality as objective and concepts as non-arbitrary. I will also seek to offer a new understanding of proof and demonstration as capable of being grounded in empirical observations rather than logical or mathematical deductions. Such an understanding benefits a philosophy of empirical reasoning such as Rand's.

My approach in this paper will employ two

different tactics. I will argue that Rand's epistemology, particularly her theory of axioms, is guilty of an internal contradiction. The internal contradiction will be explored in depth below, but can be summarized by saying that the axioms assert that they cannot be proved by reason, yet they form the foundation for all reasoning, hence all reasoning depends upon things that cannot be known by reason, and if a thing cannot be known by reason then it must be accepted on faith, therefore all reason is ultimately founded on unproven beliefs that must be accepted on faith, therefore Rand's epistemology reduces to the statement that reason is based on faith.

But I will also argue that Rand's epistemology contains what I call an "external contradiction". By "external contradiction" I mean that reality exists objectively and Rand's philosophy is not a complete and truthful account of reality as it really exists, hence one may say that Rand's philosophy is contradicted by reality. An internal contradiction happens when someone says that a thing is and also says that it is not, while an external contradiction happens when reality says that a thing is and someone says that it is not. To show Rand's external contradiction, I will offer my own unique, original theory of epistemology, based on the theory of essence. My theory describes reality as it really exists, and Rand's philosophy fails to match it. Note that my argument is not that Rand is wrong because she disagreed with my view, which is of no importance. Rather my argument is that Rand is wrong because her theory does not match reality, which can be known because my theory is a better description of reality than hers. Also, here at the beginning of my argument, I will concede that this paper is merely an introduction to my theory, and many details to my ideas exist that would require a longer discussion to be explained, such that the account given here is incomplete. I fully explain my theory elsewhere, but this paper contains enough of the gist of my ideas for the reader to undertake an evaluation of my claims regarding Rand's epistemology.

In this paper I am going to criticize Rand's position regarding axioms, by which I mean her claim that the propositions "existence exists" and "A is A," which she also referred to as "existence" and "identity," are axiomatic (Rand 1990, 55). She also considered "I exist," in other words consciousness, to be axiomatic, and although I won't deal specifically with that axiom, my argument applies to it also. Once I have established that her position on axioms is contradictory I am going to offer a different theory to replace hers. My purpose is not to show that axioms are false and therefore Objectivism falls apart. On the contrary, my purpose is to show that there are holes in Objectivist epistemology where a proof of the axioms should be, but the axioms can be proved, so that Rand's philosophy can be made much stronger and put on a more stable foundation if the holes are filled.

I do not dispute the truth of existence and identity. I merely dispute whether they are axioms. My main argument is that Rand, by claiming that existence and identity are axioms, claims that these propositions cannot be proven, but that they must be believed, and the only logical result of this is that they must be taken on faith. Nothing should be taken on faith, and I believe that those two propositions should be proved and can be proved. The problem I will seek to solve is how to prove the truth of "existence exists" and "A is A." I also believe that Rand's mistake regarding axioms trickles down and causes problems with her account of objectivity, necessity and universality.

I will begin by offering Rand's view of axioms in her own words. I will proceed to explore what Rand's axioms mean and discuss the problems with axioms and axiomatic concepts. I will look at Rand's arguments about the impossibility of rejecting the axioms without also accepting them, the non-existence of non-existence, and the stolen concept. I will then examine the difference between premises and implications. I will explain my approach to proving existence and identity by using perceptions as premises combined with essential reasoning. I will conclude by critiquing Rand's intrinsic-objective-subjective analysis and her theories of objectivity, necessity and universality.

RAND'S AXIOMS IN HER OWN WORDS

Rand's position regarding axioms is evident from a passage in John Galt's speech:

"'You cannot *prove* that you exist or that you're conscious,' they chatter, blanking out the fact that *proof* presupposes existence, consciousness and a complex chain of knowledge: the existence of something to know, of a consciousness able to know it, and of a knowledge that has learned to distinguish between such concepts as the proved and the unproved.

'When a savage who has not learned to speak declares that existence must be proved, he is asking you to prove it by means of non-existence—when he declares that your consciousness must be proved, he is asking you to prove it by means of unconsciousness—he is asking you to step into a void outside of existence and consciousness to give him proof of both—he is asking you to become a zero gaining knowledge about a zero.

'When he declares that an axiom is a matter of arbitrary choice and he doesn't choose to accept the axiom that he exists, he blanks out the fact that he has accepted it by uttering that sentence, that the only way to reject it is to shut one's mouth, expound no theories and die.

'An axiom is a statement that identifies the base of knowledge and of any further statement pertaining to that knowledge, a statement necessarily contained in all others, whether any particular speaker chooses to identify it or not. An axiom is a proposition that defeats its opponents by the fact that they have to accept it and use it in the process of any attempt to deny it'" (Rand 1957, 956).

Rand says much the same thing in her "Introduction to Objectivist Epistemology":

"Since axiomatic concepts refer to facts of reality and are not a matter of 'faith' or of man's arbitrary choice, there is a way to ascertain whether a given concept is axiomatic or not: one ascertains it by observing the fact that an axiomatic concept cannot be escaped, that it is implicit in all knowledge, that it has to be accepted and used even in the process of any attempt to deny it" (Rand 1990, 59).

We can summarize Rand's argument regarding axioms. First, she claims that the axioms cannot be proved, because proof presupposes or assumes knowledge already contained in the axioms or in an attempt at proof. Second, she attacks anyone who asks her to prove the axioms by claiming that they seek knowledge of existence from non-existence.

Third, she argues that the only way to reject the axioms is to shut up and die, and fourth, she argues that one must believe the axioms even though they cannot be proved, because it is impossible to reject them without also accepting them at the same time. We can reduce this to three basic ideas: first, the impossibility of denying the axioms, second, the non-existence of non-existence, and third, the stolen concept. I will address each of these ideas later, but first I would like to look at the theory of axioms more generally.

WHAT DO RAND'S AXIOMATIC PROPOSITIONS MEAN?

Rand believed that "existence exists" and "A is A" are axioms, but to see whether this belief is problematic we must inquire into what Rand's axiomatic propositions mean, and what it means to be an axiom (Rand 1957, 933-34). One dictionary defines "axiom" as "established or accepted principle" or "self-evident truth," and defines "self-evident" as "obvious; without the need of proof or further explanation" (Thompson 1998, 52, 826). Rand refers to Aristotle (not by name, but as "the greatest of your philosophers") when first explaining her belief in axioms, so it may be useful to examine Aristotle's understanding of axioms (Rand 1957, 934). Aristotle, in describing his theory of logic as demonstration from premises in "Posterior Analytics" Book I Chapter 2, defines an axiom as a "basic truth," i.e. a proposition in a syllogistic demonstration that has no proposition prior to it, which a pupil must know in order to learn anything even though it cannot be proved by the teacher (Aristotle 1947, 12-13). In Book I Chapter 10 he says of basic truths that they cannot be proved, and that axioms express necessary self-grounded fact and must necessarily be believed (28-29).

I would define axioms as propositions that are self-evident and form the basis of all reasoning. Rand says that "axioms are usually considered to be… fundamental, self-evident truth," and axioms are made of axiomatic concepts (Rand 1990, 55). Rand's axiomatic concepts are "primary," meaning that they are irreducible (55). She doesn't say that axioms are the beginning of all cognitive activity, but her description indicates that the purpose of the axioms is to act as "guidelines" for and to "underscore" and "delimit" all conceptual thought (59). The function of the axioms is "delimiting (knowledge) from non-existence, imagination, falsehood, etc." (261). She claims that axioms are the "base" of knowledge (Rand 1957, 956). From this it seems that Rand's axioms are the foundation for all conceptual thought in the stage of adulthood, and that Rand's axioms really are axioms in the Aristotelian sense.

What did Rand mean by the phrases "existence exists" and "A is A"? The closest Rand comes to explaining what "existence exists" means is her explanation of existence as an "axiomatic concept" as found in "Introduction to Objectivist Epistemology" (Rand 1990, 55-61). Rand claims that existence is a quality that applies to everything (56). If existence were a concept that applied to everything, then it would have no real meaning, at least no more so than the concept "everything." The phrase "existence exists" should mean more than simply "everything is everything," which is an empty statement. "Everything is everything" is an empty statement with no real meaning because the proposition "everything is everything" does not reveal new information about the term "everything."

What, then, is Rand's definition of "everything," or of "existence"? Rand doesn't believe that "existence" needs to be defined at all: "Since axiomatic concepts are identifications of irreducible primaries, the only way to define one is by means of an ostensive definition—e.g., to define 'existence,' one would have to sweep one's arm around and say: 'I mean *this*'" (41). The only problem is that "*this*" has no meaning, or if it has a meaning it is so vague and imprecise as to be useless for rational thought. Rand offers a way to refer to existence, not a definition of existence, not a description of what existence is. If it is impossible to give an intelligible definition for some idea, a definition capable of explanation, then that idea's usefulness for rational thought is highly dubious. Concretes are perceived, and so they can be defined by pointing to them; for example, I could point to an apple on my desk and say "I mean this apple." But existence and identity are abstractions, not concretes, and as such they are not directly perceived and should not be defined that way.

Of course, Rand believed that existence and identity are concepts that are perceived directly (55). My objection to this is the observation that I can see a chair, or a table, or a book, or an apple, but I do not see the concept of "existence" as such, and Rand fails to explain how one arrives at the universal abstraction "existence" via induction from perceptions of specific concretes.

"Existence exists" has a meaning. One dictionary defines "exist" as "have a place in objective reality," and defines "existence" as "all that exists" (Thompson 1998, 303). I argue that "existence" means not just being, but also having a physical, objective existence at a specific place and time, and "physical" and "objective" are not axiomatic concepts and can be debated. "Existence exists" means "reality is real," which means "everything in this world is physical and objective," and that is a statement which has content. I would argue based upon my understanding of the English language that the definition of the concept of "exist" reduces to three distinguishing characteristics: that the existing thing has the quality of being at a specific place and time, that it is made of physical substance, and that it is objective.

Rand rejected this view, arguing that "existence exists" does not reduce to "there is a physical world" (Rand 1990, 245-51). But Rand fails to adequately address two problems: first, that if "existence exists" does not mean that, then it has no meaning other than "everything is everything," which has no content, and secondly, that based on the definitions of words in the English language, the best interpretation of "existence exists" is "reality is physical and objective." Rand claims that even a primitive savage who believes in supernatural spirits has grasped that "existence exists" (248). But if that is true then we must ask: what does the savage really know? And why doesn't this knowledge prevent him from believing in spirits? If "existence" is so general, then it really is no different from saying "everything is everything," which has very little meaning.

It seems that Rand really intended "existence exists" to mean "everything is everything." She says "...what's the difference between saying 'existence exists' and 'the physical world exists'? 'Existence exists' does not specify *what* exists" (247). She also says "the concept 'existence' does not indicate what existents it subsumes: it merely underscores the primary fact that they *exist*" (59). If it is really true that "existence exists" does not specify what kinds of things exist, and is not the same as "existence is physical and objective," then Rand's axiom would not contradict the proposition "existence is made of Platonic Forms." If Rand is right then "existence exists" has virtually no content whatsoever.

Perhaps looking at the purpose of the axioms will shed light on their meaning. Rand says that axiomatic concepts enable one to know that what is true at one point in time is true at every point in time (56-57, 260-61). But how do axiomatic concepts accomplish that purpose? Her answer to that question is vague and imprecise (261). She says that the axioms' purpose is to distinguish object from subject (57, 261). But she is unclear about precisely how they do so. And she says that axioms underscore primary facts and confine knowledge to reality (261). But if "existence exists" does not say anything specific about what reality is, then how does it limit knowledge about reality? I found no intelligible explanation of how axioms accomplish these purposes in "Introduction to Objectivist Epistemology". I don't consider it a defense on Rand's part that she believed that axiomatic concepts could not be analyzed, such that the answers to my questions should be self-evident (55). If she had consistently applied the belief that axioms are incapable of analysis then she would not have been able to fill a whole section of her book on epistemology with an analysis of axiomatic concepts.

I will concede that Rand attempted to add content to her axioms in Galt's speech. She says: "existence exists—and the act of grasping that statement implies two corollary axioms: that something exists which one perceives and that one exists possessing consciousness.... To exist is to be something, as distinguished from the nothing of non-existence, it is to be an entity of a specific nature made of specific attributes. ... Reality is that which exists; the unreal does not exist..." (Rand 1957, 933-34).

She says that existence exists and that to exist

is to be something, in which case "existence exists" reduces to "everything is something." I argue that there are three problems with that reduction. First, "everything is something" might reduce to "A is A," making the first axiom redundant. Second, Rand does not give a significant analysis of what it means to be something or to have a specific nature, such that "everything is something" has little content.

My third and central problem is I believe that non-existing things are things with identities, so that "existence exists" cannot reduce to "everything is something." Regarding this analysis, I argue that "to exist" and "to be something" are different concepts. I call this analysis the Japanese Distinction, because in the Japanese language there are two completely different words for "to be" and "to exist". Japanese uses the word "desu" for "to be something" and the word "arimasu" for "to exist." (Japanese also has a third word, "imasu" which means "to be alive, to exist as a living thing".) For Rand's understanding of "existence exists" to be correct there must be no difference between the terms "to be something" and "to exist". In the English language the word "to be" has both meanings, but I argue that this is a coincidence and not a philosophical insight. This ties into Rand's idea of the "reification of the zero," which is that, according to her, only existing things are things, and nonexistent things are not really things at all, nothingness as such does not exist and is not a thing, and every truthful description of a non-existent actually reduces to a description of existents because non-existents can be known only in relation to existents (Rand 1990, 58, 60-61, 149-50).

My critique of Rand's reification of the zero argument has several parts. First, the terms "exist" and "be something" are conceptually distinguishable. One can say "a nonexistent thing" and "a non-identity" and mean two different things. One can also say of a gigantic bronze statue of Ayn Rand inside the main concourse of Grand Central Terminal in New York City that it does not exist, however it is something, and it has an identity. It has attributes of substance, appearance, and location, so one cannot say that it is not a thing. Second, it seems to me that it should be impossible to know anything about something that has no identity, so that if non-existents are not things, they would be unknowable. But one can possess some degree of knowledge about Platonic Forms, pink elephants, fictional statues of Ayn Rand, what one experiences in one's dreams, or for that matter Howard Roark, the hero of Rand's novel, who is fictional and therefore does not exist but who has a knowable personality. Rand's idea, if followed to its logical conclusion, prevents us from describing the things that don't exist. I concede that nonexistent things cannot be known except in relation to that which exists, but that doesn't mean that they have no identity.

Third, it seems to me that when something is destroyed and ceases to exist, what happens is not that it ceases to have an identity, but that it ceases to have an identity with attributes of being at that place and time in physical reality. And fourth, if Rand were right then the number "zero" would not be a thing, yet it seems to me that zero is a number and has a mathematical identity. I agree that zero does not exist, but I do not agree that it has no identity. Regarding this point Rand might have argued that zero is a concept of method, a claim that she made regarding imaginary numbers (35-36, 304-6). My dispute with numbers as concepts of method is that while the numbers may be used as a means of discovery, the numbers in themselves, e.g. the square root of negative one, must either be something or not be something, because anything else would be a contradiction. Rand's concepts of method are ambiguous as to whether they refer to things or not.

I must clarify that I believe that everything that exists is a thing, but not that everything which is a thing exists. It is difficult to make a distinction between "to exist" and "to be" because every existing thing is something. However the distinction can be done on the basis of things that don't exist, e.g. zero, and it is equally difficult, or impossible, to distinguish "to exist" from "to be objectively physical at a specific place and time," because every existing thing also has that attribute. If Platonic Forms and pink elephants are non-existing things, as I argue, then there must be something more to "exists" than merely "is something." And I posit that the something more is being physical and objective at a specific place and time.

CAN RAND'S AXIOMS BE DEBATED OR DENIED?

If it is truly impossible to debate or deny existence and identity then they are not in need of proof and Rand's axioms do not have a problem. I believe that Rand's axioms can be denied, even if they mean exactly what Rand intended them to mean and do not mean what I claimed they should mean in the previous section. In order to argue that Rand's axioms can be debated, first I will argue that linguistically it is possible to frame propositions that contradict the axioms in a manner capable of being understood and discussed, second I will argue that if the axioms cannot be proved then logic is circular reasoning, and third I will briefly discuss two famous philosophers, Plato and Derrida, whom I think would not have agreed with Rand's axioms as Rand meant them.

To argue that one can state contradictions in

a way capable of being understood and debated it may be useful to analyze the term "coherent." That term has two meanings, a common English meaning and a technical philosophical meaning, and it helps clarify the use of the word to distinguish the two meanings. The technical meaning of "coherent" is "not entailing any contradictions," or in other words, non-contradictory and logical (personal correspondence, 3 May 2009). The common meaning of "coherent," found in a dictionary, is "intelligible and articulate," and this dictionary defines "intelligible" as "able to be understood" (Thompson 1998, 158, 460). If one were to fail to carefully distinguish the two meanings one might think that incoherent propositions cannot be understood because they are contradictory, but I argue that it is possible to understand ideas that are contradictory and illogical. For example, the statement "hgteagleajrg bjergaoejighl gikhalighi" is unintelligible, whereas the statement "if you achieve knowledge of spiritual reality then it will be revealed to you that the physical world is really not the physical world" contains a contradiction, but has a meaning that is capable of being understood and debated.

If you can state contradictory propositions in a way that is intelligible then you can debate whether they are true or not, and it becomes necessary to prove that A is A in order to refute the truth of illogical propositions. Contradictory propositions that are intelligible and debatable can be formulated. It might be hard to imagine someone believing "a cat is not a cat" or "a triangle is a square circle." However, a more easily imaginable example is that a person can say "humans do not need to think in order to survive, but only need to believe in God," which Rand might have thought violated the principle "Man is Man," which violates the axiom "A is A," so Rand might have considered such a statement to be contradictory (Rand 1957, 934). Similarly one can imagine a person believing the economic theory that "inflation creates jobs," which someone else might believe to be a contradiction.

One might believe that existence and identity cannot be denied except by an insane person. It is difficult to imagine a sane person believing that A is non-A, and it is difficult to find a philosopher who openly claims that logic is useless. But a quote from Rand's Toohey speech sheds light on this: "Men have a weapon against you. Reason. So you must be very sure to take it away from them. Cut the props from under it. But be careful. Don't deny outright.... Don't say reason is evil—though some have gone that far and with astonishing success. Just say that reason is limited. That there's something above it. What? You don't have to be too clear about it either. The field's inexhaustible.   'Instinct'—'Feeling'—'Revelation'—'Divine Intuition'—'Dialectic Materialism.'... Suspend reason and you play it deuces wild. Anything goes in any manner you wish whenever you need it" (Rand 1943, 637). Rand seems to be saying that illogical thinking is widespread, and that a person can deny logic not by denying identity openly, but by believing in something besides logic. Based on this quote Rand seems to agree that logic can be denied, in fact she seems to be saying that religion and Marxism both reject reason, and if reason can be denied then it can be debated, and if it can be debated then it is in need of proof.

If "A is A" is not demonstrated then all logic is mere circular reasoning: if logic is valid because "A is A," and "A is A" is true because it is logical, then logic is a circle. It might be illogical to disbelieve that "A is A," but if logical belief in a proposition requires proof by demonstration, and "A is A" cannot be proved by demonstration, and all logic is based on belief in the proposition "A is A," then logic is not based on logic, which means, logic is not logical. To say that logic needs special rules for axioms is to concede that axioms are not logical. Either obedience to logic has an intellectual origin, in which case we have the problem of showing what that origin is, or else there is no reason to believe that one should be logical, and logic is merely arbitrary and without a foundation. My problem is more than the mere question of why one should believe in logic, although it includes that question. My inquiry is the question of where logic comes from, because if logic's foundation comes from intuition and is incapable of rational proof then it is no better than any other intellectual strategy that comes from intuition, particularly faith in God. If you cannot demonstrate that "A is A" then faith is the only basis for claiming "A is A," and if you choose to believe in unproven, undemonstrated axioms then it is mere preference whether you prefer the axiom "A is A" or the axiom "God exists," since both would be equally unproven.

I accept that it is impossible to dispute identity, the principle of non-contradiction, without being illogical, but if a person does not begin with the belief that thinking should obey the rules of logic then one has no way of knowing that it is wrong to think illogically. Rand's argument that you can only put the negation of the axioms into practice by abandoning language and committing suicide would be true only if one had to put the negations into practice in a way that was strictly consistent. But if you negate identity you no longer bind yourself to be strictly consistent, and the axioms can be denied in a way that is irrational and contradictory, but not impossible, e.g. you can believe in the physical world and in a spiritual world at the same time.

I must also note that I can think of two philosophers who might dispute Rand's axioms; I cannot be sure about what either of them would have said about Rand's axioms but I can make educated guesses. I would guess that Plato would not agree that "existence exists." He would say that existence, the perceivable world, is a mere shadow of the world of Forms, as for example in his famous cave metaphor in "Republic", or his discussion of Forms in "Phaedo" (Plato 1997, 57-73, 1132-35). And based upon what I have read about Derrida I would guess that instead of agreeing with "A is A" he would try to deconstruct that statement. Insofar as "A is A" claims to be a perfectly rational statement that perfectly represents the real world, Derrida might critique it as logocentric presence, and would dispute that any language can capture objective universal truth (Appignanesi 2007, 77-81). Because the axioms can be debated and denied we need a demonstration of them to show to doubters in order to prove to them that the axioms are true.

THE NON-EXISTENCE OF NON-EXISTENCE AND THE STOLEN CONCEPT

Before I show how it is possible to prove that existence exists and that A is A by means of essential reasoning from sensory experience, let us consider two of Rand's ideas that she offers in support of her axioms: the non-existence of non-existence and the stolen concept. Rand's non-existence of non-existence idea contains two parts: first, that the negation of existence, i.e. non-existence, doesn't exist, and therefore you have to accept existence; and second, to obtain proof of existence one would need to go outside of existence, into the realm of non-existence (Rand 1957, 956). This argument can be seen as a form of proof. But this argument is a negative proof, not a positive proof: she proves that non-existence does not exist, not that existence exists. To justify Objectivism we need positive proof. If a negative is not a positive, as Rand claims (for example, "light is not 'the absence of darkness,'.... Existence is not a negation of negatives,") then disproving the negative of "existence exists" is not the same as proving the positive "existence exists" (941-42). Rand's argument defines reality by what it is not rather than by what it is, yet her sharpest criticism of the concept of God is that it is defined only by what it is not (951-52).

Rand argues that the person who wants proof of existence wants it to come from outside of existence (956). Her general idea is that existence is all around us, so the people who doubt it want knowledge from outside of existence. This may be true for her anti-reason critic, but it is not true for the honest inquirer. Do we need to not have bodies in order to prove the truths of biology? Do we need to not contain chemicals in our bodies in order to prove the truths of chemistry? Do we need to live in a world with no geometric shapes in order to prove the truths of geometry? Does proving something within existence require you to have a point of view from outside of existence? I do not believe that it does. Why would we need non-existence in order to prove that existence exists? Critics of objectivity might claim that you would need a point of view outside of experience to claim objective knowledge, but that view is not consistent with a belief that objectivity is possible.

The stolen concept argument is that when you reject the axioms you also accept the axioms, or when you deny the axioms you use the axioms in the process, and therefore they must be accepted and can't be rejected (956). But to make this argument two things are necessary. First, you have to prove that the concepts are stolen. When this is done you establish a contradiction: you both accept and reject the axioms. Proving the theft in a persuasive manner is a big problem. It is hard to argue that the proposition "existence does not exist" contains or relies upon the proposition "existence exists," or that "A is not A" borrows the idea "A is A." The Socratic claim "I know that I know nothing" does not seem like a claim to knowledge. It seems like a claim to ignorance, with a meaning that is identical to "I know nothing" or "I do not know anything." This refutes the Randian argument that the statement "I know that I know nothing" both claims and denies knowledge, such that it entails a contradiction and accepts that knowledge is possible. I will flesh out my objection to this aspect of Rand's argument further when I discuss premises and implications in the next section.

Second, having established that a theory or idea contains a contradiction, you have to also prove that contradictions don't exist for the contradiction to be a problem. Even if you could prove that the axioms are "stolen," which would be difficult, you would still need to prove that the laws of logic should be obeyed in order for the theft to be problematic, assuming that you don't begin with an unproven law of non-contradiction. The argument that "contradictions exist" is contradictory is a circular argument: if you don't already have a proof that contradictions don't exist, then proving that "contradictions exist" is contradictory does not invalidate it, because something could exist despite being contradictory. The negative proof results in circular reasoning, and the only solution is a positive proof of "A is A."

PREMISES AND IMPLICATIONS

Nietzsche in "Twilight of the Idols" claimed that philosophers confuse the last with the first, the most abstract with the most basic, and the ultimate goal of thought with the intellectual point of origin (Nietzsche 1990, 47). This is precisely Rand's mistake. "Existence exists" and "A is A" are perhaps the most abstract propositions possible, so it makes little sense to say that thought begins with those, or that they form the base of all reasoning. It would be better to say that thought begins with induction based on the observation of the objects of perception, the most specific or "concrete," and ends with axiomatic propositions, the most general or "abstract."

I argue that Rand's theory of axioms is itself a contradiction. But I believe that her mistake is probably not random. I would conjecture that Rand made her mistake for two reasons: first, she herself did not fully understand how she had arrived at her knowledge of existence and identity, and because she did not know how to reason them, she claimed that they could not be proven. When you are sure about something but you don't know the reasons behind your knowledge, the temptation is to say that it is self-evident, which translates into the statement "I know it but I don't know why." Second, she saw that it seems as though you would have to know existence and identity in order to do any reasoning, including any reasoning that would prove them: after all, doesn't existence have to exist in order for you to be able to reason that existence exists, so wouldn't any proof be circular? (Rand 1957, 956). Regarding the first problem, I have something that Rand lacked, a proof that existence exists. But regarding the second problem we must ask: does all reasoning use those two axioms as premises?

How can you possibly reason that A is A without already knowing it? How can you engage in any reasoning or any thought without the premise that A is A and the premise that existence exists? If that were true then these ideas would have to be in the mind at birth, and they would be intuitions accepted on faith, which is precisely the problem with Rand's belief in axioms. The problem here was that Rand was confused about the difference between implications and premises. Something that is implied by an act of reason is different than something that is a premise in an act of reason. I would define an "implication" of reasoning as something that makes the reasoning true and has to be true in order for the reasoning to take place, and a "premise" of reasoning as that belief, proposition, or source of knowledge that is actually what the conclusion of the logical argument is deduced from. Identity and existence are implied by all reason, in that obviously there would be no reasoning taking place if existence did not exist in order to our brains to exist and think, and there would be no logical thought possible if things were not themselves.

But the principles of existence and identity are not what knowledge, in its origin, is actually deduced from. They are implied in all reason, but they are not the premises of all reason. Sensory experience is what all rational conclusions are ultimately reasoned from. Sense-perceived objects are the premises of all reason, since all reason begins with specific sense-perceived objects and proceeds via induction to general abstractions. Rational knowledge begins with the objects of sensory perception, and then proceeds by deriving general principles from specific perceived objects. In other words, reason integrates concepts from sense-perceived concretes. The foundation of all thought is not axioms. The foundation of thought is the specific sensory perceptions from which our concepts are formed. Rand's belief about axioms is chronologically backwards. She has us beginning with what comes only at the end. Identity and existence are not our most fundamental premises. In fact, they are the two most abstract and general concepts of all our conceptual abstract generalizations, which means they are the pinnacle of thought, not the start of thought. They are implied by all reason, but they are not the first premises of all reason.

Rand did put forward a theory of "implicit" concepts (Rand 1990, 159-62). But she seems to suggest that an implicit concept is one that is implicitly present because the material from which to integrate it is present and the mind is in the stage or process of integrating it (162). Thus, Rand's "implicit" is something in the process of being integrated, rather than something that must be true in order for reasoning to take place, and so her analysis is not precise enough to mesh with my argument. For example, I would disagree with Rand and say that the laws of physics are implicit in all reasoning (162). I would also say that an infant or young child has no awareness that existence exists or A is A, because sophisticated cognition is necessary to grasp those concepts (162). Because she was imprecise about whether an infant is actually aware of an implicit concept or not, simply saying that it is "not yet conceptualized, but it is available," it is difficult to know to what degree Rand would have disagreed with me about that (161).

I have a problem with Rand's belief that axioms are the foundation of all thought. You do not begin with the laws of logic inherent in the mind and then apply logic to the perceivable world. That is a Kantian approach to epistemology (Kant 1977, 38-49, 63-64). I believe that in the human mind as it develops for real human beings, in babies and young children, you begin with an empty mind, you experience sense-perceived objects, and then you reason from the specific perceived objects to general abstractions. You begin with sense-experience and then derive the laws of logic from that experience, using inductive reasoning. You do not begin with the laws of logic and then use them as the foundation for all cognition. Rand might have agreed with me about intellectual development because she believed that children integrate abstractions from concretes (Rand 1990, 11-13, 19-21). But if she did agree she would be contradicting herself, because beginning with the laws of logic and applying them to the world is no different from beginning with unjustified axioms and applying them to the world. Both approaches lead inexorably towards Kantian epistemology in which the laws of logic come from pure reason prior to empirical experience. The origin of reason can be either self-evident axioms or inductive reasoning from sensory experience, but not both. If axioms could be derived by inductive reason from experience then they would not be self-evident, because the observations from which they were reasoned would prove them and be the evidence supporting them.

PROOF, DEMONSTRA-TION, AND PERCEPTIONS AS PREMISES

To solve Rand's axiom problem we must discover a way to prove existence and identity. Before I offer my solution to Rand's problem, I must address the question of what "proof" is and what it means to be "demonstrated," and also what "self-evident" means. It is possible for someone to believe that nothing is logically demonstrated or proved unless the demonstration begins with premises and demonstrates that the premises prove the conclusion by means of demonstrated mathematical computations or the rules of symbolic formal logic. Such a person might believe that logic enables deductions, but that sensory experiences only enable mere inferences, but never deductions. Aristotle may have believed this: in "Posterior Analytics" Book I Chapter 31 he claims that perceptions do not provide the scientific knowledge of demonstration, because perceptions are of particulars and demonstrations are of universals (Aristotle 1947, 66-68). But in Book II Chapter 19, where Aristotle grappled with the problem of the origins of axiomatic knowledge, he states that knowledge of basic truths comes from induction from sense-perception, but he then contradicts himself by saying that it comes from intuition (106-9).

The belief that demonstration comes from logic and mathematics but not from perception is a flawed, one-sided account of reason: it accepts deductive reason as proof, but rejects inductive reason, which takes sensory experience and derives generalized abstractions and premises from that experience. If inductive reason is incapable of proof, then how can you prove the premises that logic begins with? The argument "If P then Q, P, therefore Q", or "If P then Q and R, not Q, therefore not P", and all other similar syllogisms, are mere abstract theory detached from any basis in practical reality if we lack a principle of induction capable of telling us whether P is true or false. Similarly, the logical argument "all money is made by doing work, it is good to make money, therefore it is good to let people be free to do more work," depends upon proof that making money is caused by doing work, which can only be proved via induction from sensory observations, and cannot be derived entirely from deductive logic and axioms. Unlike Rand and Aristotle, I have solved the problem of induction, by means of my theory of essence, and through empirical essential reasoning I can achieve proof and demonstrations of universals by reference to specific concrete observations.

In order to understand the theory of essential reasoning as inductive proof, we must be precise in what we mean by proof and demonstration. Something has been demonstrated, and you have proof of something, if you can point to a source of knowledge and show how you can reason a conclusion from it that is true if the source of knowledge is real. In other words, something is proven if you have evidence that proves the conclusion. The claim "a cat is in the room" can be proven if you see a cat in the room: if your perception of the cat is accurate, in other words if the cat that you see is real, then the cat itself, which you perceive, is the proof of the truth of the proposition, and you can prove it to someone else by pointing out the cat to them. The problem of induction is how we can point to one cat in the room and infer "all cats are mammals" from this one cat which we perceive, and essence is the tool that enables inductive reasoning to infer from specific to general.

It seems to me that an induction-deduction dichotomy, which could also be called a perception-logic split, is appropriate for philosophers like Kant and Descartes who want all proof to come from the analysis of concepts and who believe that logic and mathematics are pure but that the temporal physical world is muddled and illusory. But for a philosophy that believes that reason should properly be focused on the physical world and which thinks that truth can be known from empirical observations, we need to accept that induction is necessary for logic and that perceptions can be premises in deductions. I do not believe that we should draw a sharp distinction between inductive and deductive reasoning, because the two terms merely describe different phases of the same process. It is beyond the scope of this essay to prove that sense-perception provides accurate knowledge of reality which admits of absolute certainty (although I will discuss objectivity below), but it seems as though Rand accepted that it does (Rand 1957, 934).

Regarding the term "self-evident," I would argue that perceptions are the only premises that can be self-evident. I believe that a "self-evident" premise is not one that needs no proof, because something that cannot be proved would require faith in order to be known. A self-evident premise is one that contains the proof of itself within itself, in other words it proves itself just by being perceived. When I see a red apple, the apple itself is the proof that it is red, and that it exists. It contains the proof of itself within itself, therefore it is self-evident. If someone argues that the apple is not red, you simply show him the apple: the apple is the proof of its redness. One might say along these lines that "the proof is in the pudding," or as the English say, "the proof in the pudding is to be found in the eating." The proof of the thing's existence is in the thing itself, as perceived by the senses. Self-evidence is therefore a property that belongs only to specific sense-perceived objects, and not to ideas. To rephrase this in Randian terms, concretes can be self-evident, but abstractions, such as existence and identity, cannot be self-evident.

THE SOLUTION OF ESSENTIAL REASONING

My solution to Rand's axiom problem is to claim that perceived things, the objects of sensory perception, are self-evident, and universal laws such as existence and non-contradiction can be reasoned from sense experience by means of inductive reasoning. If you can reason from the experience of an apple that the apple cannot be ripe and rotten at the same time, then you can deduce a universal idea of non-contradiction from a specific instance of non-contradiction. Once derived from specific cases, universal principles can then be applied by deductive reasoning to all future instances. The propositions "existence exists" and "A is A" are best defended, not by any of Rand's arguments, but by arguing that the knowledge of existence and identity can be grasped by inductive reasoning applied to sensory experience, and that this constitutes proof.

But there is a big problem here: how do we go from specific experiences to universal principles?

How does inductive reasoning work? We can go from a specific instance to a universal law by a process that I call "the necessary consequence of the ontological essence." Some Objectivist readers might react with horror to my use of the concept of "essence," but this issue will be addressed in the following section. My solution to Rand's axiom problem depends on the idea of "essence," so I will proceed to argue that reason is best understood as relying on essences. In order to argue this I must explain my view of how essential reasoning works. It took me 120,000 words in a philosophical treatise to fully explain my theory of essences, essential reasoning and essential things, but let me try to do so now in five paragraphs. First I will define "ontological essence" as whatever quality or attribute a thing has that makes it be a particular kind of thing, and then define "the consequence of an essence" as whatever being or attributes a thing has that is caused by it having an essential attribute. In other words, a thing's essence is what makes it be that thing, and the consequence of the essence is whatever results from having that essence.

There are three ways in which an essence of a thing may result in the consequence of the essence in that thing: first, by causation; second, by requirement; and third, by containment. For example, the essence of iron will cause it to sink in a pool of water, because being iron causes a thing to be heavier than water, so that it will sink in water is a consequence of the essence of iron. Wood will require something that cuts it to be harder than wood as a means of cutting it, so the essence of being a thing that can cut wood will require the thing to be harder than wood, so that if iron cuts wood then a consequence of the essence of iron is being harder than wood. And being a metal is part of the act of being iron, because to be iron is to be a metal, so the act of being iron contains the act of being metal as a part of it, hence being metal is a consequence of the essence of being iron. From this essential reasoning we can conclude that iron is a metal, that it sinks in water, and that it is harder than wood. This will be true of all iron everywhere, such that if a thing is iron then it will do those things, and if something does not do those things then it cannot be iron.

The best example of essential reasoning comes from geometry. Reason begins with inductive reasoning: for example, you see the cover of a box, which is a red cardboard square. Your eye sends information to your brain, and this information in your brain is the perception of the red cardboard square. You analyze this information and separate the different aspects of the object. In its aspect as a red object, it is red. In its aspect as a shape with four equal sides, it is a square. By thinking this through you create the concept of a square in your brain: the processed perception becomes a concept. This is inductive reasoning. Reason can then take the essences known from perception and abstract more essential qualities from them to build knowledge of more abstract essences, such as going from the concept "square" to the concept "shape."

What makes a thing a square, in this case having four equal sides, is the essence of the square, and the consequence of that essence is whatever qualities a thing has that are caused by having that essence. You can reason the consequence of the essence of a square by thinking about the essential square, an object that has four equal sides and has no other qualities. The essential square has four right angles, because the consequence of the essence of having four equal sides is having four right angles. Having four equal sides causes a thing to have four right angles. This is deductive essential reasoning.

What is true of the essential square must be true of it because of the essence of square. Therefore what is true of the essential square must be true of all squares in the real world, because to be a square all those objects must have the square essence. If a thing did not have the essence of a square, then it would not be a square, so for a thing to be a square requires it to have the square essence, and the essence causes the consequence, so we can infer that everything that is a square has four right angles, because being a square will cause it to have four right angles. Therefore it is impossible for something to be a square and to not have four right angles. It is necessary for every square to have the consequence of the square essence, because everything that is a square must have the square essence in order to be a square, and having the square essence causes a thing to have the square consequence. By isolating the essence of a thing from a specific perceived thing and then employing essential reasoning, a person can achieve inductive reasoning and can infer general propositions from specific instances. This also shows that universal laws are obeyed because of things in themselves, not because of the structure of the mind, contrary to Kant.

Every essence is an attribute (and every attribute is an essence relative to the other non-essential attributes of that thing), and the attribute of having four equal sides is the square essence. The square essence is an aspect of squares in the real world, but the essential square does not exist: it has no specific place or time, and existing things always exist at a specific place and time. You can take essential reasoning from the essential square and apply it to new squares that you encounter. You see something square which is new to you and which you have never encountered before and yet you know instantly that it has four right angles because it is square. This is essential identification. You can take one thing as the representative of all of its kind, for example geometric reasoning from one square applied to all squares, only if you reason from the square essence of your representative square, which everything of that kind must have in order to be that kind of thing. This is why a geometric demonstration using one specific square as an example to show that every square in the universe has four right angles is effective, even though the example is just one square and there are other different squares with different measurements of the lengths of its sides. A demonstration is universal because the demonstrator deduces his proof from the square essence of the example square.

The three central mistakes that people make in their thinking are all mistakes in essential reasoning. First, some people think that what happened repeatedly in the past will always happen again in the future, confusing coincidence with necessity because they don't look for the consequence of the essence. For example, if someone sees one hundred wooden square boxes they may infer incorrectly that all squares are made of wood. This is why correlation is not causation. This is also the origin of belief in magic, e.g. someone does a dance and it rains so they conclude that doing a dance causes the sky to rain. Second, some people believe that something necessary is merely a coincidence, again because they don't grasp the consequence of the essence. This is the origin of skepticism. And third, some people believe that essential things are real, leading to a belief in a non-physical world of spiritual ideas. I posit this last mistake as the origin of Platonic Forms. This is a concise summary of my theory of essences.

If we can reason that an apple cannot be both ripe and rotten because it is an apple, then we can say that if a thing is both ripe and rotten, it is not an apple. In this way we can go from one apple to every apple, and the ontology of the thing itself, in itself, requires reality to universally obey what we believe.

If the essence requires the consequence then everything of that kind must have that consequence because to be a thing of that kind requires having that essence. It follows that if a thing did not have the consequence of the essence it could not be that kind of thing because having that essence causes that consequence and the absence of the consequence would show the absence of the essence, and so being what it is requires a thing to obey the demonstrated conclusions of essential reasoning.

The line of essential reasoning that proves "A is A" is: a contradiction is both A and not-A, there are some pairs of essences for which being one kind of thing causes a thing to not be the other kind of thing (this would be reasoned by induction from specific instances, e.g. being a dog causes a dog to not be a cat because a dog must have different organs and DNA than a cat in order to be a dog, being ripe requires an apple to have a different appearance and chemical molecular substance than a rotten apple), A and not-A are such a pair because a thing is not-A by not having the essence of A and a thing is A by having the essence of A, therefore the consequence of the essence of being A is not being non-A, therefore the essence of being A will cause the thing that is both A and non-A to cease to be non-A if it continues to be A as a consequence of being A, therefore a contradiction cannot exist.

The line of reasoning proving that "existence exists," if it means "everything (that exists) is something," is: to exist is an attribute, to have an attribute is to be a something (which is deduced from the essence of "thing," which is abstracted from perceived things,) therefore everything that exists is something.

If "existence exists" means "reality is physical and objective," it is reasoned as follows: one forms a concept of the perceivable world as physical and objective by observing perceived objects, e.g. by touching a book you learn that it is physical, by seeing a book both before and after closing your eyes you learn that it exists separately from your perception of it (because it continued to exist while not seen and therefore your vision did not create it), which means that it is objective. Because the essence of existing is being physical and objective, it follows that everything that exists, in other words existence, must be physical and objective. Another line of reasoning proves this: a thing to be perceived must be at a specific place and time, to be at a place it must exist in space, to exist in space it must be physical, to be physical it must be made of physical substance, and to be made of physical substance it must exist outside of consciousness and perception, which proves that the perceivable world exists physically and objectively.

When you reason something from some source, you can point to your source and your reasoning and say that this constitutes proof, that you have not asserted your conclusion, instead you have demonstrated your conclusion. You need only point out an apple to someone and show how you can reason that it cannot be contradictory and that it is physical and objective, and then show how to go from one apple to everything, and you have proved identity and existence to that person.

THE FLAW
IN RAND'S
INTRINSIC-
OBJECTIVE-
SUBJECTIVE
ANALYSIS

Any reader of mine who is well-versed in Rand's epistemology will now exclaim about my theory: "But that's intrinsic, not objective!" That objection is the fundamental source of Objectivism's rejection of essences (Rand 1990, 52-54). So let's deal with that objection, and see how my theory can improve Rand's account of the objective.

When Rand rejects the theory that essences are in objects rather than in the mind, she is thinking of Plato as the representative of the "intrinsic" position; her problem with Aristotle is that he is too much like Plato (141). The differences between my theory of essences and Plato's Forms come in two parts. The first difference is that Plato's Forms can never be known by sense perception, and my essences can only be known by sense-perceiving objects that have those essences, or by conceptually combining or analyzing the different essences that you have reasoned from perceived objects. The second is that Plato's Forms are in a world apart from the physical world, they are spiritual, and my essences are in the physical world, they are in physical objects. Really the essences are the physical objects, or, to phrase it more precisely, they are physical objects when they are thought about in a certain way, by focusing thought on the essential aspect of the objects. For example, the essence of a dog is every real dog thought of as dog, focusing only on what makes it a dog and not on any of its other characteristics. Also, as I mentioned, it is useful for essential reasoning to think about essential things, but an essential thing does not exist, it is merely a conceptual took for isolating and analyzing the essences of real physical things.

Thus, my essentialism does not reduce to Platonic Forms, and is fully compatible with Objectivism. Rand's objection to intrinsic essences centers on her claim that they can only be known by revelation, and that they exclude consciousness from reality (53, 141). She doesn't consider the possibility that essences could be known by perception, or that they might be in things in themselves but be known though an intellectual process such as essential reasoning which abstracts essences from perceived objects, perhaps because this might damage her intrinsic-objective-subjective idea, which is itself a contradiction. She claimed that a theory such as mine reduces thought to perception (53). But that is not true: the essence is perceived, for example you can see that a dog is a dog, but the act of abstracting the essence from a specific perceived object is an act of thought, for example it is an act of thought to go from a perceived real dog to the essential dog. In fact, her criticism here could more accurately be directed back upon herself, in the sense that she reduces thought about "existence exists" and "A is A" to perception, as if the abstract axioms were seen directly instead of being integrated from inductive reason.

Being, what makes a thing be what it is, what can be called essence, is either in things in themselves, outside of the mind, which Rand rejected as "intrinsic," or else it is in the mind, in which case it is subjective. There is nothing in between. For being to be both in things and in the mind is a contradiction. And if being is in the mind, but is based on reality, then what precisely is it in reality that it is based on? Rand writes that "*A concept is a mental integration of two or more units possessing the same distinguishing characteristic(s), with their particular measurements omitted*" (13). Either the "distinguishing characteristic" is in the thing, which Rand rejects as "intrinsic," or it is in the mind, in which case Rand's epistemology reduces to subjectivism. Rand also says that the definition of a concept must be by its most essential characteristic, the one that causes and explains all or most other defining characteristics (45, 71, 230-31, 238-39, 304). If this quality of being essential is merely in our minds and not in reality, if it is epistemological rather than metaphysical, then how is our concept not subjective?

Rand's "objective" is a contradictory compromise between "intrinsic" and "subjective," an attempt to claim that being is somehow in between reality and the mind. The truth is that being is in reality but is known by the mind, but Rand's "objective" does not accomplish this.

She says that essence is "epistemological," not "metaphysical," but essence is another word for being or what makes a thing be what it is, therefore Rand's statement reduces to the claim that being is in the mind, not in reality (52). If we are going to be rational then we must conclude that the "intrinsic" position is what makes objectivity possible. This also reflects what is visible, for example, what makes a square be a square is its four equal sides, and this is in the square, not in our minds: it is metaphysical, but it is known by epistemology. Rand's intrinsic-objective-subjective account contradicts what she says elsewhere, namely that the attributes of entities are metaphysical, not epistemological (277-79). A square's essence, as square, is its attribute of having four equal sides, and every being's essence is merely whichever attribute it has that is essential as that type of thing.

When Rand claims that the objective is between the intrinsic and the subjective, the implication is that the objective is in the mind rather than intrinsic to external objects, but yet it is still somehow related to something outside the mind. That is a contradiction. If essence is in the mind but is related to reality, then what in reality is it related to? If definitions refer to essential characteristics, what are these characteristics if not essences? Either the defining characteristic of a thing is in the thing itself, which Rand rejected as "intrinsic," or it is in the mind, in which case it is subjective. Rand asks "to what precisely do concepts refer in reality? Do they refer to something real, something that exists —or are they merely inventions of man's mind, arbitrary constructs or loose approximations that cannot claim to represent knowledge?" (1). Yet this, the question of what concepts refer to in reality, is what Rand fails to answer, and what she cannot answer because she rejects the idea of essences. An essence is a thing's identity as a specific kind of thing which is in the thing itself, so if there are no essences then concepts have nothing to refer to.

If we reject Rand's intrinsic-objective-subjective analysis, then what becomes of objectivity? A good theory of objectivity was put forward by Aristotelian philosopher Mortimer J. Adler in his "Ten Philosophical Mistakes" (Adler 1996, 5-82). Adler argued that the problem of objectivity is an interrelated conceptual and linguistic mistake. The word that is missing from the discussion is "of," which denotes the object of a subject. When I see an apple, the apple is not a perception. The apple is the object of a perception. The perception is in my mind, whereas the apple that I see is out in the external world. When I think about a dog, the concept of "dog" is in my head, but the dog itself is out in the world, if it exists, or if the dog doesn't exist, then it isn't anywhere, and I am thinking about something that doesn't exist.

Perceived things and thought-about essences are the objects of consciousness, whereas the perceptions and concepts are the means by which I perceive or think about things. Perceptions and concepts are in my mind, whereas what I see and think about is in reality. If I am thinking about a square, the concept of "square" is in my mind, but the essential square, the object of thought, does not exist, and I am really thinking about all the squares that exist as such, as squares. Adler argued that since perceptions and concepts are in the mind, if we see perceptions and we think about concepts, we become trapped in subjectivism and we can only see and know what is within the mind. I extend that argument by claiming that what we perceive is objective reality precisely because what we perceive is that which we perceive, not the means by which we perceive it, and this fact is itself perceptually verifiable, e.g. when you look at a book you see the book, not your eyes.

If we use "of," if we are aware that what is in the mind is only the means by which we perceive and think, rather than the objects of perception and the contents of thought, we can escape from this problem. Rand, who advocated a belief in an objective reality, should have said that we perceive an objective reality, a world outside of our mind, a world separate from the mind and independent of the mind. But she didn't understand how to put this belief on a solid logical footing. Because Rand claimed that the things that we see are perceptions made of sensations, and that things such as existence and identity and everything else abstract are concepts, her epistemology reduces to subjectivism (Rand 1990, 5, 10). But the problem is easily fixed: simply know that existence is not a concept, it is a thing to which a certain concept refers, and the things that you see are not your perceptions, they are the things in objective reality which the perceptions in your mind are your means of perceiving. Being itself is in things in themselves, but our concepts of beings are in our minds.

This enables us to say things that Rand rejected, but should have said: that concepts and perceptions physically exist in our brains, but refer to objects outside of our brains, that the mind reduces to the brain, that the self reduces to the body, and that the mind-body relationship is a question whose answer lies in philosophy, not science (154, 290). This also clears up Rand's confusion and imprecision over whether concepts physically exist as concretes or not (154-58). I would argue, contrary to Rand, that a mind cannot understand itself or the world around it in any meaningful way until it grasps its relationship to its body, the relationship of consciousness to self. And once you deduce that perceptions come from the impact of external objects on your body's sense organs, you can reason that everything that you perceive exists objectively.

OTHER PROBLEMS WITH RAND'S EPISTEMOLOGY

Rand might have challenged me to show in what way the essence is not arbitrarily defined, but I don't consider that to be a problem. The essences are in things in themselves, but which essence you are thinking about is a matter of your choice. A thing is a set of attributes, and essential reasoning chooses one attribute and then reasons the consequence of the essence which then applies to everything which has that attribute. For example, if you have a red cardboard square, thinking about it as a square rather than as a red thing is a choice, but the four sides producing four right angles is not a choice. Rand's disciple Peikoff might have objected that if non-essential qualities are contingent rather than necessary then we enter the problem of the "analytic-synthetic dichotomy," but I disagree with that as well (115). A thing's non-essential qualities are contingent relative to the essential quality, but are absolute when the thing is considered as a whole. Rand seems to think that an Aristotelian essence is a physical object within a thing that gives it identity, as if there were an organ inside of humans that made them human, and each organ is identical (139). I dispute this. An essence is an attribute of an object, such that the details of what I do and what you do may differ, but our act of being human, as such, is identical, in that we are both beings which think and have human DNA and generally human-shaped bodies. If there was nothing identical between us then we would not both be humans.

Where are the universal laws of logic, such as identity? Where are metaphysical facts? If they exist in this world, where are they so that we can point to them and look at them and touch them, or if they exist in a different world, how is that not a non-physical world of spirit, which contradicts Rand's metaphysics? Why are the laws of logic necessary, and why are they true everywhere and at every time? Rand says that things act a certain way because a thing "must act in accordance with its nature," but where precisely is a thing's "nature"? (287-88). Is it in the thing itself, or in some other plane of existence? What exactly is a thing's "nature"? And if one goes from concretes to universals by means of measurement-omission, precisely how does the mind go from a concrete measurement to a universal measurement-omission? (11-12). Specifically, how does the mind know that any measurement may be substituted for the omitted measure-ments? (18). What are the "characteristics" that de-termines whether a concrete is included in a concept or not, which Rand seems to admit are the basis of conceptual categorization, if not an essence in the things in themselves? (17).

Rand's theory has no answers for these ques-tions, but my theory does. Metaphysical facts and the laws of logic do not exist separately from the physical world. They are the essences in physical ob-jects. The essence of "thing," the essence of a thing as a thing, in other words a thing as such, requires it to be itself and to not be not itself. A thing must have the essence of a thing in order to be a thing, so the essence requires obedience to the laws of logic, and the metaphysical fact of identity is the essence of a thing. This is why propositions stated as meta-physical facts are necessary for all things of that kind. For example, a consequence of the essence of water is that it is a liquid when it is at room tem-perature, so all water, not just some water, is a liquid at room temperature. A thing's essence as that thing is its "nature," that is why it behaves in a certain way, because it has that being. The essence of water is being H2O, so if a scientist reasons that water is liquid at room temperature because of its chemical composition, then this is proved as a universal truth for all water. For a thing to be water it must be H2O, and being H2O causes a thing to be a liquid at room temperature, so the essence of water will require all water to be liquid at room temperature.

The essences are in the things in this world. Essences are the things of this world thought about using essential reasoning, so they exist physically in our world, and not in a separate Platonic world of spirit. But it is the essence, not the mind's essential reasoning, which requires that things in reality obey the metaphysical facts and act according to their nature. Necessity comes from the essence itself. The essence requires the consequence of the essence, and having that essence is being that thing, so being the thing will cause the consequence. Essential reasoning enables the mind to go from specific things to universals, because induction derives a concept of the essence of a type of thing from one, a few, or a group of some real things with that essence, and deduction then reveals the consequence of that essence which must be true for all things with that essence.

Rand admits that concepts must match "essential" characteristics, and that "essential" characteristics exist, but claims that this is the case because cognitive efficiency and practicality dictate it (52, 65, 70-72). It would make more sense and be less arbitrary if the justification was that the essential characteristics actually exist, in other words if essences exist. Rand acknowledges that definitions should be based on "fundamental" characteristics which cause or explain most other characteristics (42, 44-45). If this is the case, how is the fundamental characteristic not an intrinsic essence if it is in things in themselves, and if it is not in things in themselves, then how are definitions based on objective reality? Rand posited rules for the formation of concepts, but the same critique applies to her rules as well: if a black swan is a swan because of attributes of the black swan itself, then those attributes are an essence of "swan," and if it is a swan merely because it is mentally useful for humans to classify it as one, then the concept of "swan" is hopelessly subjective (70-73).

RETHINKING RANDIAN NECESSITY AND UNIVERSALITY

My theory also corrects a problem in Rand's account of necessity, which is based on her theory of the metaphysical vs. the man-made (299). For her the metaphysical could not be different than it is because God did not create the Universe, but the man-made, because man has free will, could have been different. My problem with her analysis is, first, that she says that metaphysical facts were not created by God, but she does not explain where they come from, and second, that while she explains why metaphysical facts are necessary, she does not explain why it is necessary for the objects in reality to obey those metaphysical facts, she offers no detailed mechanism for explaining how necessity functions. My theory explains where metaphysical facts come from, e.g. "squares have four right angles" comes from the essence of squares. My theory of essences provides a clear, understandable mechanism for how necessity is created: because a thing must have the essence in order to be that kind of thing, and the essence causes the consequence as a result of having that essence, everything of that kind must have the consequence because it is what it is, e.g. every square must necessarily have four right angles because it is a square, and if it did not have four right angles then it could not have the square essence and it would not be a square.

My analysis extends to solve another contradiction in Rand's epistemology, her belief that all knowledge is contextual (42-43). Rand's thoughts on necessity as it relates to her metaphysical vs. man-made distinction and universality as it relates to contextual knowledge are captured in a bit of dialogue about water in "Introduction to Objectivist Epistemology" (295-301). A "professor" asks her how we know that water boils at a certain temperature, and why we know that all water boils at this temperature rather than merely all the water that we have known in previous experience. She begins by saying: "By whether you can or cannot establish a causal connection between what you have determined to be the essential characteristic of water and the fact that it boils at a certain temperature" (295). I fully agree with this statement, and this quote supports my theory of essences rather than Rand's own intrinsic-objective-subjective idea. But when asked how to establish the connection, Rand ducks the question by saying that the answer lies in science, not philosophy, because it involves molecular chemistry. When pressed on why molecular knowledge matters, she says that it is simply because we have gained more knowledge. This I disagree with: it is not merely more knowledge, rather it is knowledge of cause and effect, of the consequence of the essence of water, and this is where necessity and universality come from.

Rand, without this idea, then posits that water boiling at that temperature is necessary because it is metaphysical and not man-made, and says that this knowledge about water applies only to specific cases, and could be proven wrong if we were to learn more knowledge, because all knowledge is contextual (296, 298). It is true that there are certain specifics to the case of water boiling at a certain temperature, but these all must be considered in essential reasoning, to arrive at the essence whose consequence you want to reason. In other words, water is an essence, water at a high altitude is another more specific essence, water at a high altitude with salt in it is an even more specific essence, and each essence has its own consequence. Thus, when you have reasoned the consequence of an essence, you can say that your knowledge is necessary and universal, without any possible exceptions, regardless of any new "context." But when Rand claims that not just some, but all knowledge is contextual, she paves the road to skepticism or relativism. For her position to be applied logically, all knowledge is merely relative to one's context, and everything that one knows, literally everything, could be disproved by a new context. This is a form of skepticism since it makes absolute knowledge impossible, and it is relativism because it makes all knowledge relative to one's context.

Rand claims that a new context will never contradict previous knowledge, but she never proves why this will be the case (43-45). If your context changes and forces you to give up on knowledge or definitions that you had previously held to be true, it would seem that your previous knowledge has been disproved. She claims that mathematical knowledge is not contextual, but this leads to an analytic-synthetic split: math would be analytical, empirical science would be synthetic (202-3).

Rand's contextual knowledge is a contradictory concession to those who claim that empirical reason cannot provide absolute certainty. If all knowledge is contextual then no knowledge can claim to be truly universal. The solution is to see the difference between more knowledge and consequence of the essence knowledge: the former can be overturned by still more knowledge, whereas the latter is necessary and universal, in all cases. Essential knowledge is not just more knowledge. It is a special kind of knowledge.

Our theory of necessity and universality is of the utmost importance. In my opinion the great appeal of Kant is that he offers a comprehensive theory of necessity and universality. Kant claimed that necessity is created because the mind applies the laws of science to everything that it experiences with no exceptions (Kant 1977, 63-64). Thus Kantian subjectivism creates universality. If we are to challenge Kant's supremacy we will need an account of necessity and universality that comes from things in themselves, which is impossible if we accept Rand's intrinsic-objective-subjective analysis.

CONCLUSION TO RAND'S AXIOM PROBLEM

For Rand, because concepts are "merely… our way of organizing concretes," without reference to essence in things in themselves, it is impossible for Rand to justify universal knowledge, or to claim knowledge of things in the future (Rand 1990, 307). Nowhere in "Introduction to Objectivist Epistemology" does Rand explain how, if concepts are not based on essences, they are not arbitrary, nor how, if they are merely groupings of concretes from previous experience, do they offer knowledge of the concretes that one is going to experience in the future. If concepts are merely a way to mentally organize concretes, then how is conceptual reason capable of proof? Rand's concepts, just because they are "open-ended," do not enable her to prove truths about the future, because her concepts do not refer to essences in concretes and so she has no basis for knowing that concretes in the future will resemble concretes from the past (17, 27, 66). She claims to have solved the "problem of universals," but her answers are problematic (1-3).

Because things in themselves are required to have the essence in order to be that kind of thing, since they would not be that kind of thing if they did not have the essence, and the essence causes the consequence, my essences offer universal knowledge. Only essential reasoning enables your knowledge of the present and the past to produce conclusive, demonstrated knowledge, in other words proof, about the future and the things that you have not yet experienced. My theory also enables reasoning that is purely empirical, in other words, which is purely the result of deductions from sense perceptions. Essential reasoning solves the problem of induction. Rand's axioms are assumptions dressed up in a fancy name, and as soon as you base your reasoning on unreasoned assumptions instead of perceptions, you can no longer claim to base your knowledge on empirical observation of the perceivable world. Indeed, reliance on the axioms is based on faith in the axioms, and Rand's theory of axioms contradicts her commitment to reason.

My theory will give an epistemological foundation to Rand's metaphysical, ethical and political ideas that is stronger and more logical than the theory of axioms. My theory will also introduce a more logical conception of objectivity, necessity and universality than is found in Rand's writings. I agree with Rand's vision of reality as objective and as something that can be understood and mastered by the reasoning human mind, but the details of her epistemology betray and contradict that vision. Fortunately we have a solution to Rand's axiom problem.

Let me add a concluding postscript to this paper. When I first submitted it to "The Journal of Ayn Rand Studies," it was rejected for two reasons: first, because the reviewer asserted that I was accusing Rand not of an internal contradiction, but merely of disagreeing with my personal epistemology, and second, because I did not fully explicate my epistemic theory of essences alluded to in the paper. The conception of this paper as incomplete is a straw man. The rest of this book explains the details of my philosophical beliefs, but the above presentation gives enough of the gist of my ideas for my critique of Rand to be thoroughly understood. Secondly, my argument is undeniably one based on Rand's own internal self-contradiction, as well as her external contradictions.

Rand believed in reason and rejected faith, but she accepted the axioms without reasoned proof that the axioms are true. If the reader of this paper considers the natural, reasonable proposition that something which cannot be proven by reason must be accepted on faith, since the origin of any idea is either reason or faith, then it follows that Rand's premises collapse into a contradiction, in that reason is based on axioms and axioms must be accepted on faith, hence reason is based on faith. Merely disagreeing with my argument, in the absence of a well-reasoned critique, does not refute my argument. Disagreement does make clear whether the reader of this paper possesses blind faith in the ideas of Ayn Rand, or whether he or she is willing to check Rand's premises and question the Randian philosophy using a serious philosophical methodology.

REFERENCES:

Correspondence

Chris Matthew Sciabarra, 3 May 2009

Publications

Adler, Mortimer J. 1996. Ten Philosophical Mistakes. New York: Touchstone.

Appignanesi, Richard and Chris Garratt. 2007. Introducing Postmodernism. Cambridge: Icon.

Aristotle. 1947. Introduction to Aristotle. Edited by Richard McKeon. New York: Random House.

Kant, Immanuel. 1977. Prolegomena to Any Future Metaphysics That Will Be Able to Come Forward as Science. Translated by Paul Carus, revised by James W. Ellington. Indianapolis: Hackett.

Nietzsche, Friedrich. 1990. Twilight of the Idols/ The Anti-Christ. Translated by R.J. Hollingdale. New York: Penguin.

Plato. 1997. Complete Works. Edited by John M. Cooper. Indianapolis: Hackett.

Rand, Ayn. 1957. Atlas Shrugged. New York: Signet.

___. 1990. Introduction to Objectivist Epistemology. 2nd ed. Edited by Harry Binswanger and Leonard Peikoff. New York: Meridian.

___. 1943. The Fountainhead. New York: Signet.

Thompson, Della, ed. 1998. The Oxford Dictionary of Current English. New York: Oxford University Press.

END

ABOUT THE AUTHOR

Russell Hasan

Russell Hasan is the author of these books:

NONFICTION:

A System of Legal Logic: Using Aristotle, Ayn Rand, and Analytical Philosophy to Understand the Law, Interpret Cases, and Win in Litigation (A Scholarly Monograph)

If P Then Q: Why Philosophy Can Teach You How to Think and Help You Live a Happy Life By the Methods of Applying Logic to Solve the Problems in Your Life and Achieve Success (A Scholarly Monograph)

The Power of Objectivism: Ayn Rand and John Galt and Atlas Shrugged and The Morality of Life, Intelligence, Greed, Selfishness, Rationality, Individuality, Integrity, Capitalism, Desire, and Freedom

What They Won't Tell You About Objectivism:

Thoughts on the Objectivist Philosophy in the Post-Randian Era

The Apple of Knowledge: Introducing the Philosophical Scientific Method and Pure Empirical Essential Reasoning

Golden Rule Libertarianism: A Defense of Freedom in Social, Economic, and Legal Policy

On Moral Psychology and Moral Philosophy: Towards a New Theory of Emotions, Motivations, and Ethics, Using the Insight that Emotions Pay Moral Debts and Moral Credits Owed to Self and Loved Ones (also published under the alternate first edition title On Forgiveness)

XYAB Economics: A GOLD Libertarian Analysis of Money, Trade, and Freedom

A Law and Economics Approach to Litigation Costs: The Proportionality Test for E-Discovery Law (A Scholarly Monograph)

FICTION:

The Paradise Machine

The Magic Key Cards

Fallen Angel and Other Contemporary Coming-of-

Age Romance Short Stories

The Golden Wand Trilogy (also published as a three-book set called The Wand)

Project Utopia: A Libertarian Science Fiction Anthology

The Office of Heavenly Restitution: A Fantasy Fiction Anthology

The Prince, The Girl and The Revolution: A Science Fiction Fairy Tale

Rob Seablue and The Eye of Tantalus

Russell Hasan (pronouns: He, him, his) is a graduate of Vassar College and graduated with Honors from the University of Connecticut School of Law. He is a proud member of the LGBTQIA+ community and an equally proud member of the Libertarian Party. Mr. Hasan has served as a member of the LGBTQ Rights Committee of the New York City Bar Association, and has been Vice Chair of the Libertarian Party Affiliate of Fairfield County, Connecticut. He loves coffee and chewing gum, and enjoys watching sports, comedies, and science fiction/fantasy tv shows and movies. His favorite books are Atlas Shrugged and The Fountainhead and his favorite movies are Star Wars and The Matrix.

Made in United States
Orlando, FL
01 July 2022

19339526R00041